KIDS' TRAVEL GUIDE

USA

FlyingKids Presents:

KIDS' TRAVEL GUIDE
USA

Author: Shiela H. Leon

Editor: Carma Graber

Designer: Slavisa Zivkovic

Cover design: Francesca Guido

Illustrations: Slavisa Zivkovic, Francesca Guido

Visit us @ www.theflyingkids.com

Contact us: leonardo@theflyingkids.com

ISBN 978-1499677850

TABLE OF CONTENTS

This is the only page for parents in this book ...

Dear Parents,

If you bought this book, you're probably planning a **family trip** with your **kids**.

You are spending a lot of time and money in the hopes that this family vacation will be **pleasant** and **fun**. You would like your children **to learn** a little about the country you visit—its **geography**, **history**, unique **culture**, **traditions**, and more. And you hope they will always remember the trip as a very **special experience**.

The reality is often quite different. Parents find themselves frustrated as they **struggle to convince** their kids to join a tour or visit a landmark, while the kids just want to stay in and watch TV. On the road, the children are glued to their mobile devices instead of enjoying the new sights and scenery—or they complain and constantly ask, "**When are we going to get there**?" Many parents are disappointed after they return home and discover that their kids **don't remember much about the trip** and the new things they learned.

That's exactly why *Kids' Travel Guide — USA* was created.

With *Kids' Travel Guide — USA*, young children become **researchers** and **active participants** in the trip. They learn fun facts about history and culture; they play games and take quizzes. This helps kids—and parents—**enjoy the trip a lot more**!

How does it work?

A family trip is fun. But **difficulties** can arise when children are not in their **natural environment**. *Kids' Travel Guide — USA* takes this into account and supports children as they **get ready** for the trip, **visit** new places, **learn** new things, and finally, **return** home.

The *Kids' Travel Guide — USA* does this by helping children to **prepare for the trip** and know what to expect. During the trip, kids will read **relevant facts** about the United States and get advice on how to adapt to new situations. *Kids' Travel Guide — USA* includes **puzzles**, **tasks** to complete, useful **tips**, and other **recommendations** along the way. All of this encourages children to experiment, explore, and be more involved in the family's activities—as well as to learn new information and make memories throughout the trip. In addition, kids are asked to **document** and write about their experiences during the trip, so that when you return home, they will have a **memoir** that will be fun to look at and reread **again and again**.

Kids' Travel Guide — USA offers general information about the USA, so it is useful **regardless** of the city or part of the country you plan to visit. It includes basic geography; flags, symbols, and coins; basic history; and colorful facts about culture and customs in the United States.

If you are traveling to the US you may also want to get the **city series,** which includes San Francisco, Los Angeles, San Diego, New York City, and more. This series focuses on the city itself—its history and culture, and all its interesting and unique attractions.

Ready for a new experience?
Have a nice trip and have fun!

Leonardo

Hi, kids!

If you are reading this book, it means you are lucky—you are going to the **United States** **of America!**

You probably already know the places you will visit, and you may have noticed that your parents are getting ready for the journey. They have bought travel guides, looked for information on the Internet, and printed pages of information. They are talking to friends and people who have already visited the USA in order to learn about it and know what to do, where to go, and when ... But this book is not just another guidebook for your parents.

This book is for you only the young traveler.

First and foremost, meet Leonardo, your very own personal guide on this trip. Leonardo has visited many places around the world. (Guess how he got there?) He will be with you throughout the book and the trip. Leonardo will tell you all about the places you will visit—it is always good to learn a little bit about the country and its history beforehand. He will provide many ideas, quizzes, tips, and other surprises. Leonardo will accompany you while you are packing and leaving home. He will stay in the hotel with you (don't worry, it does not cost more money)! And he will see the sights with you until you return home.

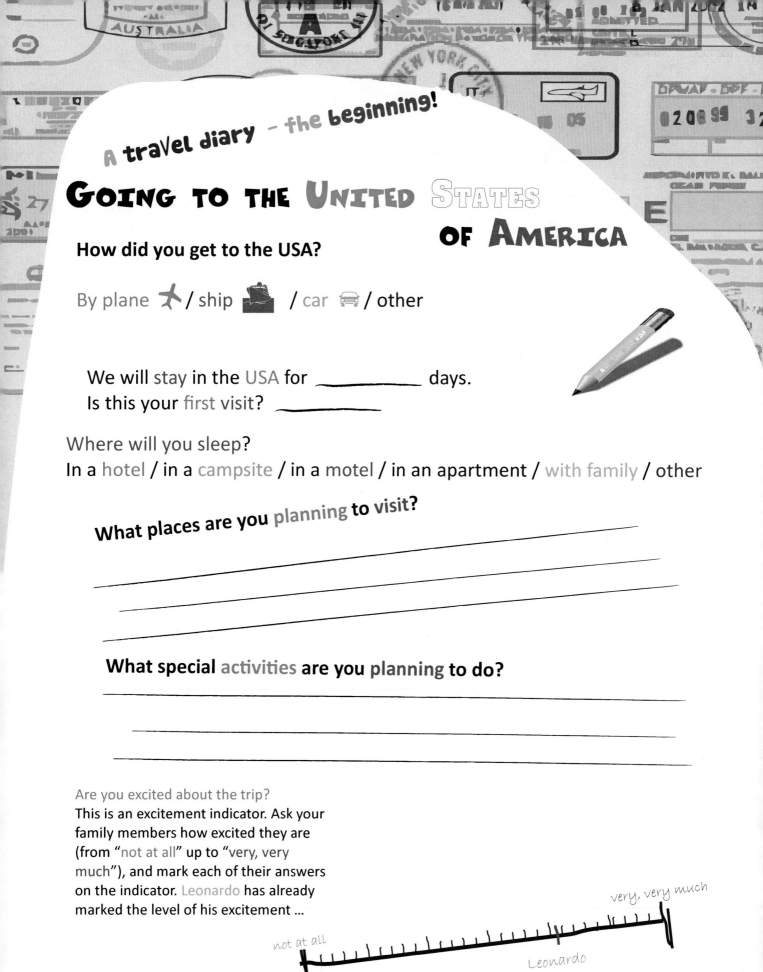

A travel diary - the beginning!

GOING TO THE UNITED STATES
OF AMERICA

How did you get to the USA?

By plane ✈ / ship 🚢 / car 🚗 / other

We will stay in the USA for _____ days.
Is this your first visit? _____

Where will you sleep?
In a hotel / in a campsite / in a motel / in an apartment / with family / other

What places are you planning to visit?

_____
_____
_____

What special activities are you planning to do?

_____
_____
_____

Are you excited about the trip?
This is an excitement indicator. Ask your family members how excited they are (from "not at all" up to "very, very much"), and mark each of their answers on the indicator. Leonardo has already marked the level of his excitement ...

very, very much

not at all

Leonardo

Who is traveling?

Write down the names of the family members traveling with you and their answers to the questions.

Name: _____

Age: _____

Has he or she visited the USA before? yes / no

WHAT IS THE MOST EXCITING THING ABOUT YOUR UPCOMING TRIP?

_____
_____

Name: _____

Age: _____

Has he or she visited the USA before? yes / no

WHAT IS THE MOST EXCITING THING ABOUT YOUR UPCOMING TRIP?

_____
_____

Name: _____

Age: _____

Has he or she visited the USA before? yes / no

WHAT IS THE MOST EXCITING THING ABOUT YOUR UPCOMING TRIP?

_____
_____

Name: _____

Age: _____

Has he or she visited the USA before? yes / no

WHAT IS THE MOST EXCITING THING ABOUT YOUR UPCOMING TRIP?

_____
_____

Name: _____

Age: _____

Has he or she visited the USA before? yes / no

WHAT IS THE MOST EXCITING THING ABOUT YOUR UPCOMING TRIP?

_____
_____

Name: _____

Age: _____

Has he or she visited the USA before? yes / no

WHAT IS THE MOST EXCITING THING ABOUT YOUR UPCOMING TRIP?

_____
_____

Preparations at home – do not forget …!

Mom or Dad will take care of packing clothes (how many pairs of pants, which comb to take …). Leonardo will only tell you the stuff he thinks you might want to take on your trip to THE USA.

Here's the Packing List Leonardo made for you. You can check off each item as you pack it:

✹ *Kids' Travel Guide —* USA*—of course* ✔

✹ COMFORTABLE WALKING SHOES

✹ A RAINCOAT
(ONE THAT FOLDS UP IS BEST—SOMETIMES IT RAINS WITHOUT WARNING …)

✹ A HAT
(AND SUNGLASSES, IF YOU WANT)

✹ PENS AND PENCILS

✹ CRAYONS AND MARKERS
(IT IS ALWAYS NICE TO COLOR AND PAINT.)

✹ A NOTEBOOK OR WRITING PAD
(YOU CAN USE IT FOR GAMES OR WRITING, OR TO DRAW OR DOODLE IN WHEN YOU'RE BORED …)

✹ A BOOK TO READ

✹ YOUR SMARTPHONE/TABLET OR CAMERA

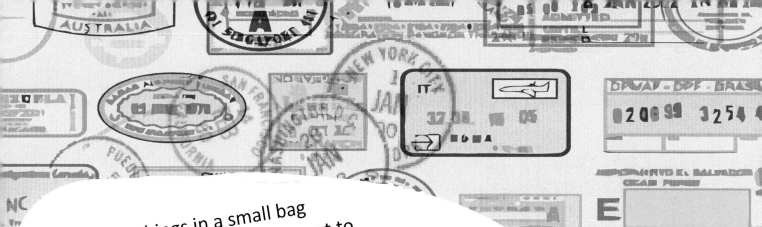

Pack your things in a small bag (or backpack). You may also want to take these things:

✈ Snacks, fruit, candy, and chewing gum. If you are flying, it can help a lot during takeoff and landing, when there's pressure in your ears 😦.

✈ Some games you can play while sitting down: electronic games, booklets of crossword puzzles, connect-the-numbers (or connect-the-dots), etc.

 Now let's see if you can find 12 items you should take on a trip in this word search puzzle:

□ Leonardo
□ walking shoes
□ hat
□ raincoat
□ crayons
□ book
□ pencil
□ camera
☑ snacks
□ fruit
□ patience
□ good mood

P	A	T	I	E	N	C	E	A	W	F	G
E	L	R	T	S	G	Y	J	W	A	T	O
Q	E	Y	U	Y	K	Z	K	M	L	W	O
H	O	S	N	A	S	N	Y	S	K	G	D
A	N	R	Z	C	P	E	N	C	I	L	M
C	A	M	E	R	A	A	W	G	N	E	O
R	R	A	I	N	C	O	A	T	G	Q	O
Y	D	S	G	I	R	K	Z	K	S	H	D
S	O	A	C	O	A	E	T	K	H	A	T
F	R	U	I	T	Y	Q	O	V	O	D	A
B	O	O	K	F	O	H	Z	K	E	R	T
T	K	Z	K	A	N	S	I	E	S	Y	U
O	V	I	E	S	S	S	N	A	C	K	S	P

Let's meet the United States of America

The United States of America (USA) is a huge and unique country that does almost everything in a big way! It is the third largest country in the world 😲. You can think of the US as more than just a country. In fact, it is a federation* of 50 small countries, called states, that are all united under one main government.

> * Federation: many countries or states united into one group. Each of the countries is independent and governs itself, but they are all part of a bigger government that takes care of the needs and problems they share.

Have you heard of New York City? Orlando? Boston? Las Vegas? What about the Grand Canyon and Disneyland?

Indeed, the United States has amazing attractions of all kinds—from beautiful parks and cities to interesting and surprising landmarks and events, as well as people from all cultures around the world—in short, everything you need to travel, have fun, and find lots of new and fascinating things!

How big is the US?

From the East Coast to the West Coast, it's about 3,000 miles (or nearly 5,000 kilometers). That's a long way!

The US has all kinds of weather too. In the North, winter is very cold with lots of snow.

In the southern states, it stays warmer and hardly ever snows.

The US Southwest is a desert area, and in the Northwest, it's damp and rainy a lot of the time.

What is the weather like in the place you're visiting?

Quizzes!

We've said that the United States is the third largest country in the world. Do you know what the two biggest countries are (*in amount of land*)?

1 _____ 2 _____

This is the world map.

Where is the United States on the map? Can you draw a line around the US?

The compass rose/borders

The compass rose is a drawing that shows the directions: North-South-East-West. North is always at the top of the map, and from that you can know the rest of the directions. When you need to find a place, you can use a compass. The compass shows the compass rose, and the needle always points north. This helps you to navigate and figure out where places are, so you can get from one place to another.

North

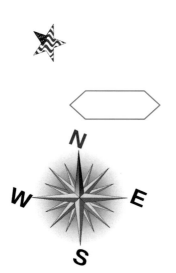

Mark the three missing directions in the blank squares.

Borders

Lines on the map show the borders between countries or states. These lines mark the beginning and end of each country or state's land. When you're traveling, you'll see different kinds of borders: Natural borders are made by rivers, mountains, oceans, etc. When there is no natural border between countries or states, sometimes a fence or a gateway marks the border, and sometimes the border is just shown by a sign.

Look at the map. What forms the borders of the United States?

In the north: _____   In the south: _____

On the east: _____   On the west: _____

About the US states

This is a map of the USA that shows all the states.

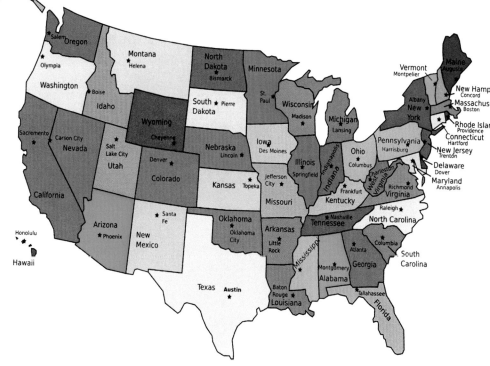

Try to find the state that has the most neighboring states.
How many other states touch its borders?

Quizzes!

What state has the longest name?

Did you know?
The state of Alaska is nearer to Russia
than to the other US states .

In fact, the states of Alaska and Hawaii aren't connected to the
other 48 states at all. Hawaii, in the Pacific Ocean, is the only
US state completely made up of islands.

Did you know?
The United States has more than
300 million people !

How many people live in your country? _____

ANSWERS

ANSWERS

Massachusetts, North Carolina, South Carolina

Actually, there are two states:
Missouri and Tennessee are each
bordered by eight other states.

New York City is the biggest US city, and more than eight million people live there. The second biggest city is Los Angeles, with more than three million residents.

Did you know?

In the state of Montana, there are three times as many cows as there are people .

Leonardo looked at a map of the United States, but all the names of the states had been shortened to two letters. Now Leonardo can't figure out the name of each state. Can you help him?

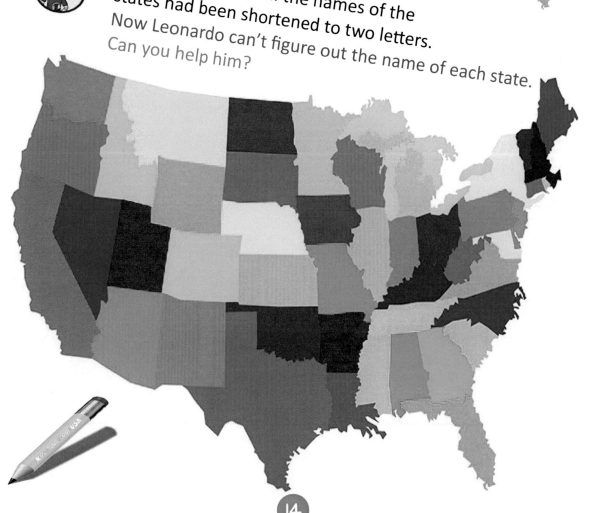

Five important facts about the United States got mixed up.
Can you connect each question to the right answer?

First US State   California   more than 34 million people

Newest State   Wyoming   half a million people

State with the Most People   New York   over 8 million people

State with the Least People Hawaii   since 1787

Biggest City in the USA   Delaware   since 1959

Did you know?

Alaska's coastline is longer than the coastlines of all the other 49 US states put together.

Quizzes!

What is the capital of the United States?

1. Las Vegas
2. Washington, DC
3. Boston
4. New York

ANSWER
Washington, DC

First US State — Delaware — since 1787
Newest State — Hawaii — since 1959
State with the Most People — California — more than 34 million people
State with the Least People — Wyoming — half a million people
Biggest City in the USA — New York — over 8 million people

About the US capital — Washington, DC

Each of the 50 states in the United States has its own capital. The national capital of all 50 states is Washington, DC. It is named after the first president of the United States, George Washington. The "DC" stands for "District of Columbia." "DC" helps people know you are talking about the capital city and not the state of Washington. Washington, DC, sits on the banks of the Potomac River, next to the states of Virginia and Maryland.

All the most important decisions of the United States are made in Washington, DC. At the center of the city stands the impressive Capitol Building. This is where the Congress meets. Each state sends representatives to Congress, and together they make the US laws and the decisions about relationships with other countries. The leader of the United States is the president. The president and the president's family live in a huge house called the White House, and the president takes care of the problems of the country and sometimes the whole world.

This is the seal of the District of Columbia.

This is the flag of Washington, DC.

Do you recognize the building in the picture?
Who lives there ?

ANSWER
This is the White House, where the United States President and first family live—and even their cats and dogs!

About US monuments and national parks

National monuments were built to honor important events and people in US history.

Have you heard about monuments in the US? Leonardo will tell you about a famous one 😃 : Mount Rushmore, in the state of South Dakota, is one of the most popular monuments in the United States. It's a sculpture of the heads of four US Presidents, carved into the side of the mountain by hundreds of workers—who used dynamite, jackhammers, chisels, and drills. The heads are 60 feet (18 meters) tall 😮 .

Quizzes!

Do you know which US Presidents are seen on Mount Rushmore?

Another of America's favorite monuments, the Statue of Liberty, was a birthday gift to the US from France on July 4, 1884. Standing in New York Harbor, Lady Liberty is a symbol of freedom and democracy. The statue is as tall as a 15-story building, and she lifts her torch to welcome visitors, immigrants, and US citizens returning from abroad.

ANSWER
George Washington, Thomas Jefferson, Theodore Roosevelt, and Abraham Lincoln

Did you know?

Inside the Statue of Liberty there are 354 steps.

354 steps

US national parks

US national parks are large areas of land set aside for the people to enjoy. Nearly 60 national parks protect America's scenery, wildlife, and historic places.

Quizzes!

What was the first national park in the US?

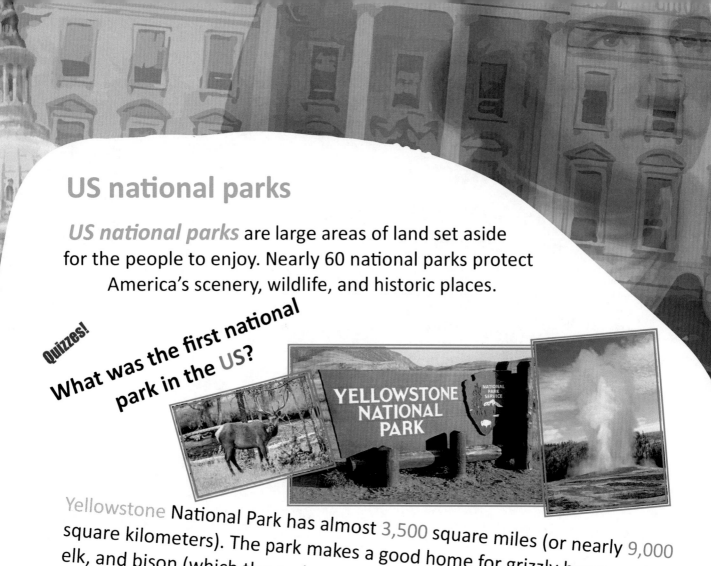

Yellowstone National Park has almost 3,500 square miles (or nearly 9,000 square kilometers). The park makes a good home for grizzly bears, wolves, elk, and bison (which the early settlers called "buffalo").

Yellowstone National Park has more geysers* than anywhere else on earth. The most famous geyser, Old Faithful, shoots water around 130 feet (40 meters 😮) into the air about 17 times a day.

*A geyser is a hot spring that is under pressure and spurts columns of water and steam into the air.

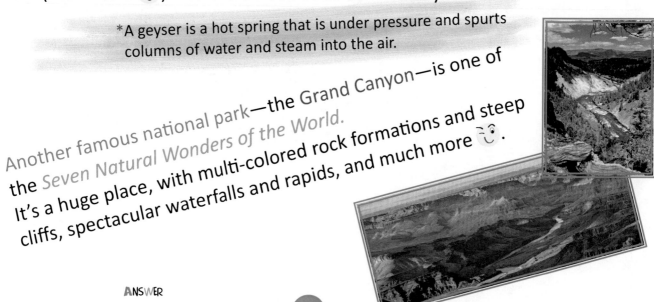

Another famous national park—the Grand Canyon—is one of the *Seven Natural Wonders of the World.* It's a huge place, with multi-colored rock formations and steep cliffs, spectacular waterfalls and rapids, and much more 😉.

ANSWER
Yellowstone

About flags, symbols, and coins

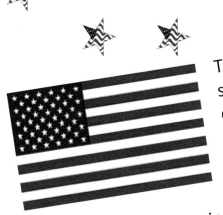

This is the United States flag. It has 13 red-and-white stripes and a blue rectangle with 50 stars. The flag was designed in 1777. At that time, the country was made up of 13 colonies that were fighting the Revolutionary War to win their independence from Great Britain. The flag had one stripe and one star for each colony.

After the war, the colonies became the United States, and many more states joined the US over the years. (Read about this in the chapter "Once upon a Time.") The 13 stripes on the flag have always stayed the same—to stand for the original 13 colonies. But a new star was added to the flag every time a new state joined the United States, and the flag now has 50 stars.

This is the United States flag as seen in 1777.

How were the colors for the flag chosen?

Each color has a meaning:

Red stands for hardiness (being strong and sturdy) and valor (bravery).

White stands for purity and innocence.

Blue stands for vigilance (watching out for danger), perseverance (sticking with something even when it's hard), and justice.

The symbol of the
United States — the Great Seal

Look at the Seal: In the center, there's an eagle—a symbol for strength, courage, and freedom. The eagle holds 13 arrows in one hand. Do you remember what the number 13 stands for? The 13 original colonies of the United States 😊. In the other hand, the eagle holds an olive branch.

The olive branch is a symbol of peace, and the arrows stand for war. You can see that the eagle is looking toward the olive branch—and this shows that the US wants peace more than war.

The eagle is holding a saying written in Latin. It means "Out of Many, One"—one nation created from 13 colonies and the people of many races, religions, and countries. Above the eagle, there's a white cloud around golden rays and a blue sky with 13 stars. A shield with 13 red-and-white stripes covers the eagle's chest.

The Great Seal is put on foreign treaties and other papers signed by the US President.

Did you know?

The bald eagle is the national bird of the United States.

Can you find 10 differences between the two pictures of the Great Seal?

How can you buy things in the United States?

If you want to buy something in the United States, you have to have US dollars. One dollar is equal to 100 pennies or 100 cents.

Did you know?

"Dollar" comes from a Czech word. Hundreds of years ago in the Czech Republic, silver from the mines was made into coins. They called the coins *Joachimsthaler*, or *taler* for short. That sounded like "dollar" in English, and the British people started calling any large silver foreign coin a dollar. The United States decided to use the word "dollar" as the name for its money in 1785. All European countries measure the worth of their money by comparing it to the value of the US dollar.

Americans have "nicknames" for their money ⌣. Can you find the name that goes with each coin?

Draw a line between the coin and its name.

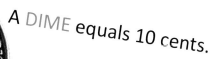
A DIME equals 10 cents.

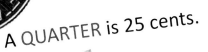
A QUARTER is 25 cents.

21

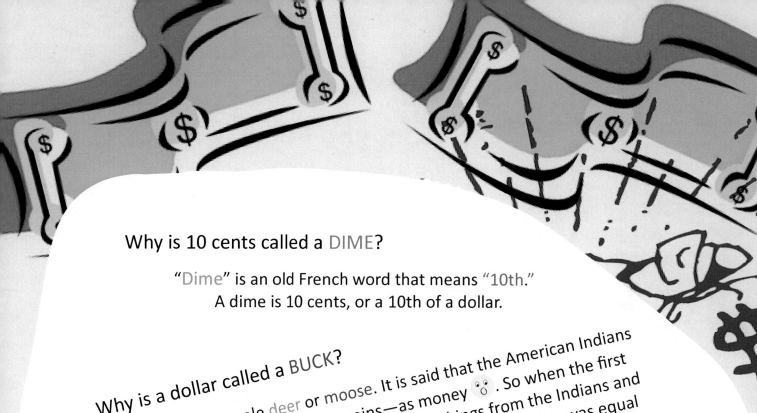

Why is 10 cents called a DIME?

"Dime" is an old French word that means "10th."
A dime is 10 cents, or a 10th of a dollar.

Why is a dollar called a BUCK?

A "buck" is a male deer or moose. It is said that the American Indians used the skins of bucks—not coins—as money. So when the first Europeans came to America, they bought things from the Indians and sold them things using buckskins for money. One buckskin was equal to one dollar. Even when the US started using coins and bills for money, people still called dollars "bucks."

Try to find these words in the following word search puzzle:

- [ ] dollar
- [ ] Great Seal
- [ ] Washington
- [ ] dime
- [ ] capital
- [ ] buck
- [ ] Leonardo
- [ ] USA flag
- [✓] quarter

q	u	a	r	t	e	r	c	u	n
l	e	o	n	a	r	d	o	d	g
a	f	h	t	v	b	i	a	d	e
k	j	s	x	b	h	m	w	o	v
g	r	e	a	t	s	e	a	l	c
u	e	c	a	p	i	t	a	l	c
z	d	i	u	s	a	f	l	a	g
e	v	b	u	c	k	o	a	r	a
w	a	s	h	i	n	g	t	o	n

Once upon a time: some history ...

Did you ever hear of Christopher Columbus? Do you know who came to the Boston Tea Party? What is the Fourth of July? The US has a long, rich, and very interesting history!

Picture of Christopher Columbus

US history starts with Christopher Columbus, the man who discovered America. Well, the truth is he probably wasn't the first European to come to the shores of America 😕. But his visit in 1492 is the first time we have proof that a European set foot on American soil. In fact, Christopher Columbus was really trying to sail around the world to get to Asia on the other side 😊.

Did you know?

Until the day he died, Christopher Columbus did not know that he came to America. He was sure he had landed on the coast of India 😊.

And where did America get its name?

America is named after the Italian explorer Amerigo Vespucci.

Like Columbus, he was trying to sail around the world to get to Asia. But Amerigo Vespucci knew he had instead found a "New World" (different from Europe, or the "Old World"). In 1507, a German man was drawing the first world map that showed the New World. He decided to name it "America" after "Amerigo." He wrote the name on the map, and after that, everyone started calling it America.

After Columbus, the Spaniards came to America. They were the first Europeans to stay and live in America. French traders came next, and then the Dutch and English. Within 200 years, England had 13 colonies along the East Coast and had taken over most of the French and Spanish colonies.

Quizzes!

Do you remember how many stripes are on the American flag and why?
(You can go back to "Flags, Symbols, and Coins" if you need a reminder 🤭.)

Did you know?

Some people didn't come to America by choice. Africans were brought to the US to be slaves 😔.

Why did people leave Europe and come to America?

They had many good reasons. Some were looking for religious freedom. In America no one told them what religion to follow. Other people wanted a chance to have lots of farmland so they could support their families better. Others thought they would find jewels and gold! And many came for the adventure. But they were all looking for new opportunity, a better life, and the freedom to live the way they wanted.

So how did 13 British colonies become a giant country like the USA???

In America, everything was new and different from Europe. When the first Europeans got here, the land was covered with a thick, deep forest. They had to chop down the trees so they could build cities and plant crops. As the colonies grew, the people developed their own customs, and they began to think of themselves as Americans instead of Europeans. But even though they lived in America, the people in the 13 colonies had to pay high taxes to the British government in Europe. That made them really, really mad 😮.

Have you ever been to a tea party?

Have you heard about the Boston Tea Party?

Well, it wasn't exactly a party—but some people wore costumes! It happened in 1773. Three British ships came to Boston Harbor filled with tea. (The early Americans really liked tea!) The British government said the colonists had to pay a tax before the tea could be unloaded from the ships. The colonists didn't think that was fair. So in the middle of the night, hundreds of them dressed up like Indians and went to the ships, and they dumped all the tea into the water!

This was called the Boston Tea Party. It's an important event in history because it started the Americans' fight for independence from the British, and it led to the Revolutionary War.

So what kind of tea party would you rather go to ૮ૢ ?

Don't worry, there's a happy ending.

Ten months later, the colonies formed their own Continental Congress. And what happened then? Nearly three years after the Boston Tea Party, on the historic day July 4, 1776, the 13 colonies signed the Declaration of Independence from the British government. Ever since, this day has been celebrated as Independence Day.

Signing of the Declaration of Independence

Quizzes!

So what is Independence Day called in the United States? _____

Did you know?

After the Declaration of Independence, Americans still had to fight the Revolutionary War to become free from British rule. The British didn't accept that the United States was an independent country until seven years later 😠.

And how do Americans celebrate their Independence Day?

It's a day of fun for everyone, with joyful parades, picnics, and big fireworks shows at night.

How do you celebrate Independence Day in your country? _____

Is it the same or **different** from how the United States celebrates? _____

Did you know?

In Leonardo's country, they celebrate Independence Day by playing trumpets and drums all night 😊.

About American culture and Americans

So far we've been talking about the United States and its history, but we haven't talked about the people who live there—the Americans 😊.

What are they like? What do they like to do in their free time? What music do they like to listen to? What do they like to talk about?

Americans are very generous, polite, and kind. They work hard and follow the rules. They are patient when they have to stand in long lines at restaurants, shops, and events.

Americans are also very patriotic.* They fly their flag proudly in many places—at government offices, schools, homes, and stores. The national song, or anthem, is played at public events, and the Americans usually stand up, put their hands on their hearts, and take off their hats while it plays.

* Patriots are proud of their country, loyal to it, and willing to fight for it.

Did you know?

All Americans pledge allegiance to the flag and know they should never let the flag touch the ground.

Quizzes!

People have many nicknames for the USA. Leonardo made a list of these names, but he got a little mixed up. Help him figure out which nicknames are real and which ones are mistakes:

ANSWERS

Uncle Sam, The New World, The States, The Land of Opportunity, Yankeeland

★ Uncle Sam
★ The New World
★ The land of choice
★ The Land of Opportunity
★ The States
★ The 50 states federation
★ Yankeeland
★ The Johnathan

What kind of music do Americans ♫ like to hear? ♩

Soul music, jazz, pop, rock, country, hip-hop—even classical ... Anything goes! Americans love music, musicians, singers, bands, and orchestras.

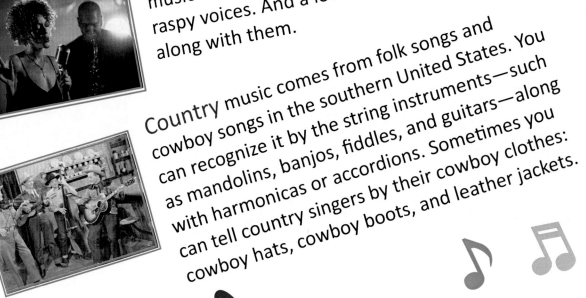

Jazz was invented in America. It began during slavery when the African music of the slaves met European music—interesting meeting! Both sides combined their rhythms, and jazz was born. Jazz has some basic rules—and a lot of improvisation (making up the music as you play).

Soul music also comes from the US. How does soul music sound? Soul singers have deep and sometimes raspy voices. And a lot of times, a saxophone "sings" along with them.

Country music comes from folk songs and cowboy songs in the southern United States. You can recognize it by the string instruments—such as mandolins, banjos, fiddles, and guitars—along with harmonicas or accordions. Sometimes you can tell country singers by their cowboy clothes: cowboy hats, cowboy boots, and leather jackets.

Famous music stars in America

America has some of the world's biggest music stars of all time. (Some of them your parents know, and some of them you probably know.) Have you heard of Elvis Presley, Michael Jackson, Madonna, or Britney Spears?

 What other American singers or bands do you know? _____

Who knows why it's called pop music?

Quizzes!

Who knows who these singers are?

1

2

3

4

1 _____ 3 _____

2 _____ 4 _____

It's a short name for "popular" music.

ANSWERS

ANSWERS
1 Michael Jackson, 2 Madonna,
3 Britney Spears, 4 Elvis Presley

The American MTV Video Music Awards are one of the most important events in the world of music. Everyone who works in the music industry and all their fans are eager to see who wins. But the Grammy Awards are the most important event in the US music scene and worldwide. The show is broadcast live throughout the world, and awards are given to musicians in 30 different music styles.

Hollywood and American films

Who knows where Hollywood is?

ANSWER ---- Los Angeles, California

How can we talk about America without talking about movie stars, movies, and ... Hollywood!

America is the film capital of the world, and many, many movies are made in the US every year.

And the Oscar goes to…

Lots of the movies you see in theaters were produced in Hollywood. One of the biggest movie studios there is called Universal Studios. You can visit it and learn how some of your favorite films were made.

The Oscars, or Academy Awards, are the US awards for film. Winners get a small statue that is known by its nickname, "Oscar." Millions and millions of movie lovers in more than 200 countries watch this glamorous awards show on live TV. Awards are given in up to 25 categories, including best movie of the year and best foreign-language film ♨.

Do you have a favorite American movie star? _____

What are your favorite movies? _____

Television

Americans watch more TV than any other country in the world. Many of the TV series that you and your parents know are American. Americans love TV shows of all kinds: action shows, romantic dramas, talk shows, soap operas, reality shows, comedies (called "sitcoms"—short for "situation comedies"), and more.

When did all this start?

The first television programs were shown in the US in 1928. And the first professional football game aired in 1939. Since then many successful TV series and sports games have been broadcast to the whole world.

The Emmy is the most important award in the world of TV. The cast and crew members of every TV show want to win Emmy Awards.

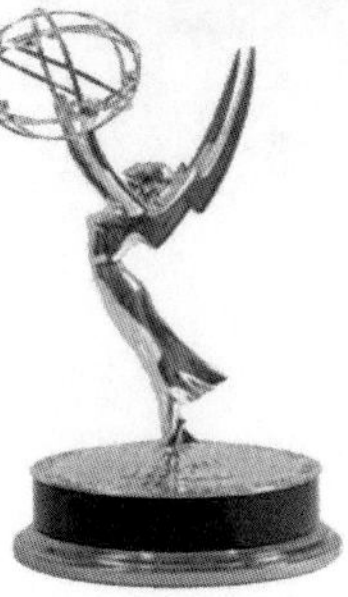

What programs or American TV series are your favorites?

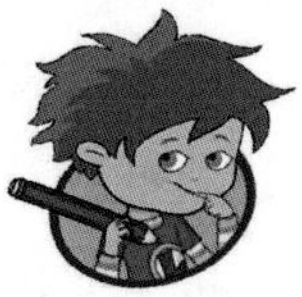

1 ____________ 3 ____________

2 ____________ 4 ____________

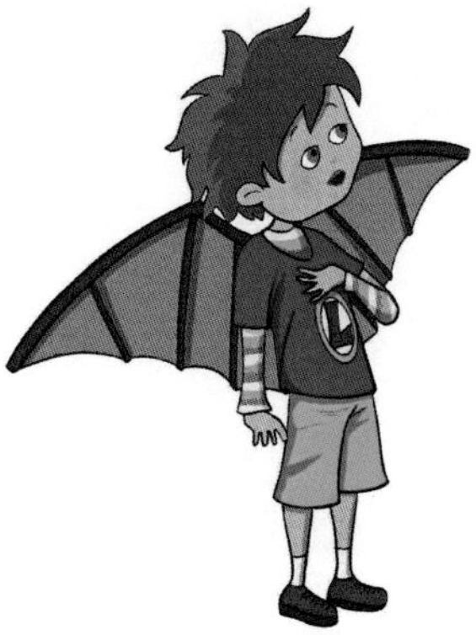

Leonardo is a talented guy. He won all three prizes in America, but somehow he forgot what each prize was for and what it was called.

Can you help him figure it out?

1

2

3

ANSWERS

1 Grammy (music)
2 Oscar (film)
3 Emmy (television)

1 ____________ 2 ____________

3 ____________

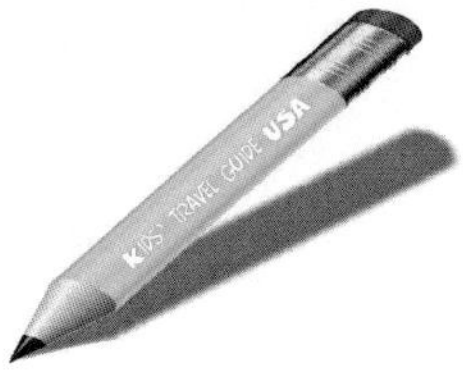

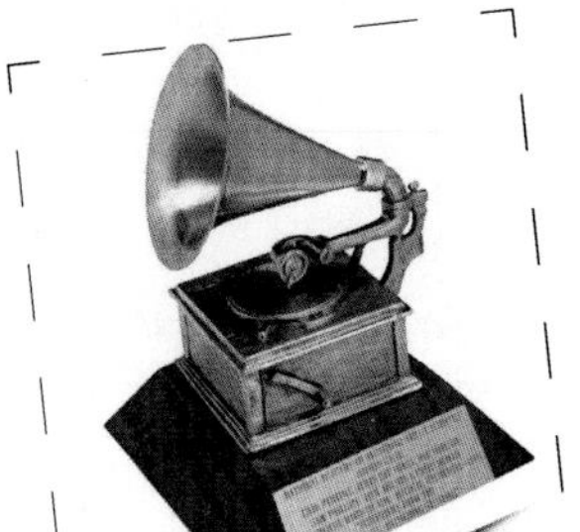

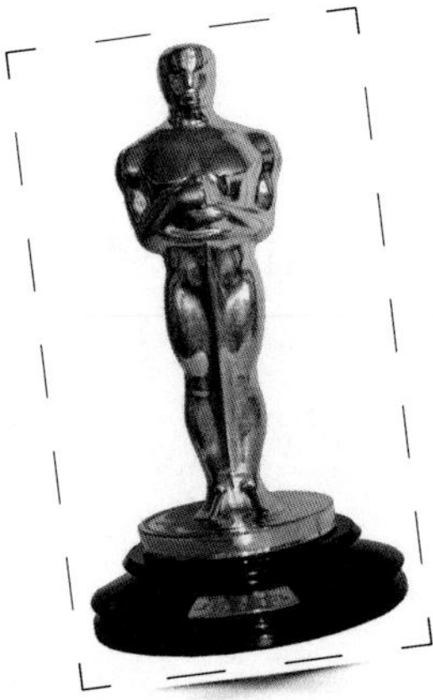

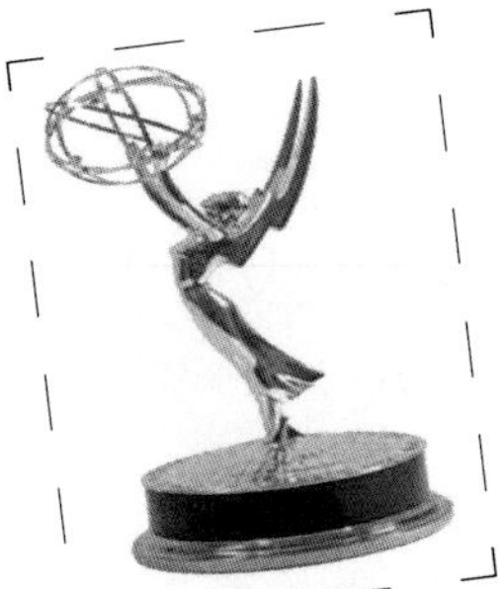

Sports

Have you heard of the *Los Angeles Lakers, New York Yankees*, or *Buffalo Bills* ☺ ? The most popular sports in the United States are baseball, football, ice hockey, and basketball.

Do you know sports?
Let's see! Connect the picture to the right sport:

 1

 2

 3

 4

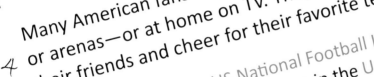

Many American fans watch sports games in big stadiums or arenas—or at home on TV. They get together with their friends and cheer for their favorite team.

The championship game of the US National Football League is called the SUPER BOWL. This is the most popular sports event in the United States! Half of the country watches it on live TV—often at SUPER BOWL parties where people eat snacks and enjoy the game.

Baseball was invented in the US in 1845 from an English game called rounders. Baseball is called "AMERICA'S NATIONAL PASTIME." The championship is a series of games called the World Series, played every fall.

From left to right: 2, 4, 3, 1

ANSWERS

If you meet an American ...

Just follow some basic rules—and you'll get along great!

Most of the time, you will call Americans by their first names. But if someone is introduced to you as Mr. Brown, be sure to call him Mr. Brown unless he tells you to use his first name 😉.

It is usually better not to talk to people you don't know, but if you need to talk to a police officer on the street, or a clerk in a store, or another adult you don't know, just call them "Sir" or "Ma'am."

Americans will often ask, "How are you?" A good way to answer is: "I'm fine, thank you, and how are you?" When you leave, you can say: "Have a nice day!"

Can you guess which one of these people is American?

Let's see! Connect each picture to the right country's traditional dress:

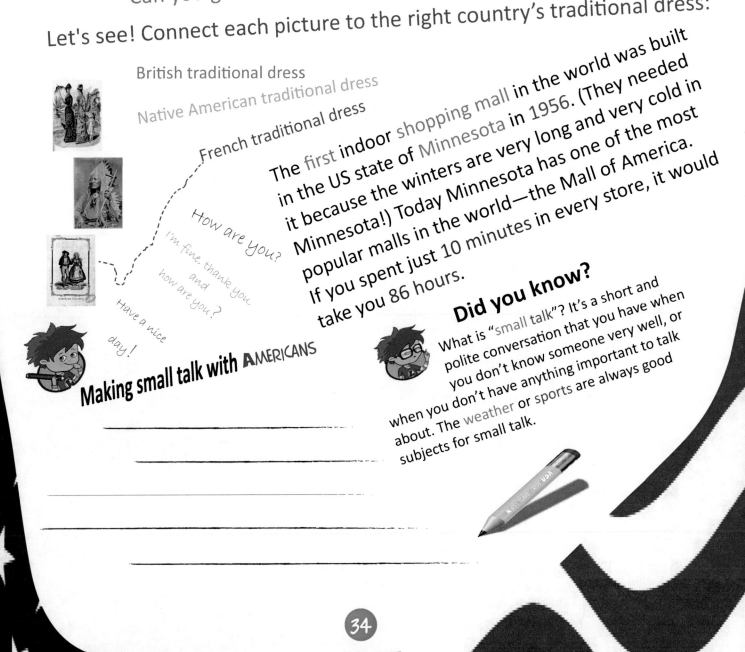

British traditional dress

Native American traditional dress

French traditional dress

How are you?

I'm fine, thank you, and how are you?

Have a nice day!

Making small talk with AMERICANS

The first indoor shopping mall in the world was built in the US state of Minnesota in 1956. (They needed it because the winters are very long and very cold in Minnesota!) Today Minnesota has one of the most popular malls in the world—the Mall of America. If you spent just 10 minutes in every store, it would take you 86 hours.

Did you know?

What is "small talk"? It's a short and polite conversation that you have when you don't know someone very well, or when you don't have anything important to talk about. The weather or sports are always good subjects for small talk.

Let eat something — about American food

When you travel, you will often find new foods that are strange to you. But when you visit the United States, you may find a lot of foods you have heard of or even eaten before. America has it all! Who doesn't know hamburgers, pizza, macaroni and cheese, pancakes, and hot dogs?

Anyone hungry ☺ ?

Where will you eat in the USA?

Americans love to eat at fast-food chains, family restaurants, cafeterias, and coffee shops.

How about playing a game with your family? Who can name the most fast-food restaurants?

And the winner is: _____

Where else do Americans love to eat? In a diner, of course!

Diners are family restaurants that serve American food. You can eat at a table or sit on a stool at the counter. Many diners are open 24 hours a day. So if you like a burger at two in the morning, or eggs and bacon for supper, just head to the diner.

The deli is another place that Americans love to eat. It's very popular in the big cities. At a deli, you'll find big bowls or trays of food behind a glass counter. Just tell them what you want, and they will put the food on a plate or in a little box for you. You can usually sit down to eat, or you can take your box of food with you and eat it later—Americans call that getting food "to go". *(Don't forget to ask for a fork, knife, and spoon.)*

Why is it called a deli?

"Deli" is short for "delicatessen". You can also think of it as short for "delicious".

What will you eat in the USA?

BREAKFAST
DESSERT
LUNCH
DINNER

Remember when we told you that people from all over the world came to live in the US? Well, they all brought their favorite foods with them. That's why there are so many different kinds of food in the United States. Because you'll find foods from all around the world, it's hard to say exactly which foods are "American." But pizza, hamburgers, hot dogs, peanut butter, and ice cream sundaes have all become popular American food.

Have you heard the saying "As American as apple pie"?

What's for BREAKFAST

In America, you have to make a lot of room for breakfast. The menu usually includes these choices:

🍽 A stack of pancakes with maple syrup

🍽 Hash brown potatoes on the side

🍽 A bowl of cereal with milk

🍽 Triangular-shaped toast

🍽 An omelet, or fried eggs with ham, sausage, or bacon

🍸 Orange juice or grapefruit juice

What would you choose to eat?
Check and write your favorite dish. _____

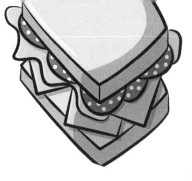

Did you know?

More breakfast cereal is made in Battle Creek, Michigan, than in any other city in the world.

And what's for LUNCH?

Soups, salads, roast beef sandwiches, chicken sandwiches, peanut butter sandwiches, and hamburgers on buns with french fries or potato chips—these are all things Americans like to eat for lunch. Lunch is usually a smaller meal than dinner—or supper (both names are used for the evening meal).

Dinner at a restaurant usually starts out with an appetizer.* After that comes soup or a small salad.

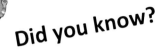

* What is an appetizer? It is a small plate of food you eat before your meal, while you're waiting for the rest of your food to be prepared.

The main course is called the entrée. Steak, fish, chicken, and ribs with barbecue sauce are all popular foods at dinner. You may get a baked potato, a stack of french fries, or some mashed potatoes (whipped potatoes) with your meal ☺.

And for DESSERT!

Leonardo listed his favorite American desserts for you.
Which one do you like best?

Chocolate Fudge Cake

Apple Pie

Cheesecake

Milkshake

Hot Fudge Sundae
(Scoops of ice cream with
hot chocolate sauce poured on top)

Brownie

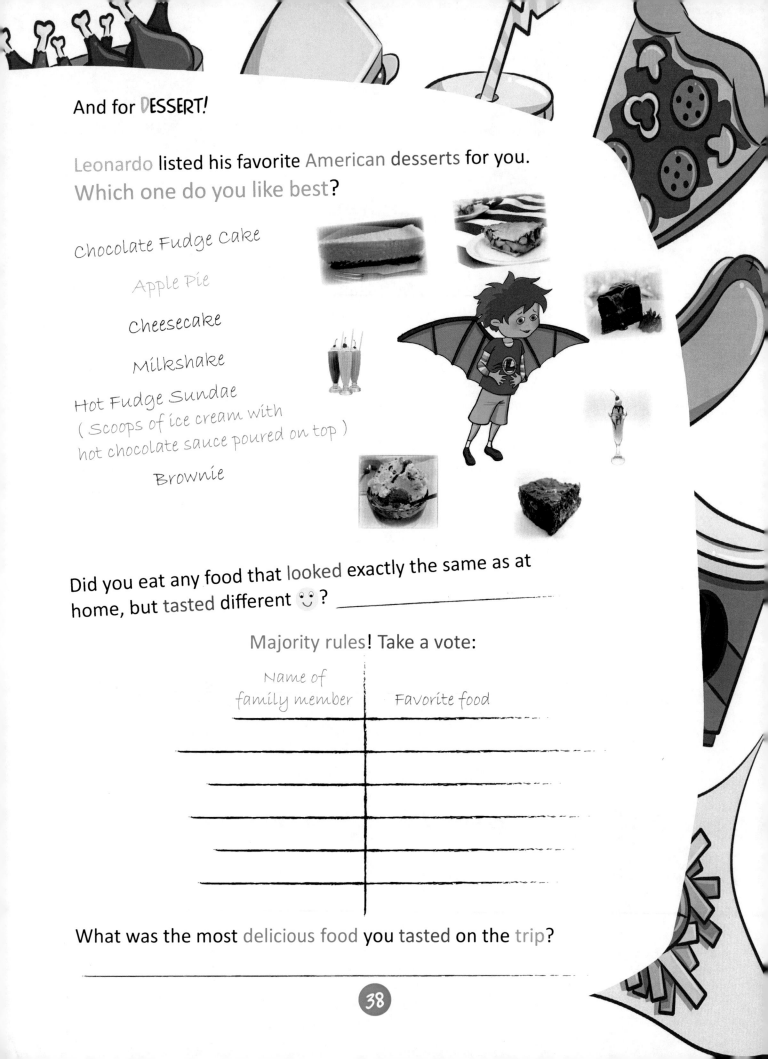

Did you eat any food that looked exactly the same as at
home, but tasted different 😊? _____

Majority rules! Take a vote:

Name of family member	Favorite food

What was the most delicious food you tasted on the trip?

_____

TRIVIAQUIZ: What do you know? about the USA?

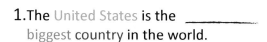

1. The United States is the _____ biggest country in the world.

   A. Fifth
   B. Second
   C. Third
   D. Most

2. Who was the first president of the United States?
   A. George Washington
   B. George Bush
   C. Christopher Columbus
   D. Indiana Jones

3. How many stars are on the US flag today?
   A. 13
   B. 50
   C. 52
   D. 40

4. Which of these is America's national bird?
   A. Red hawk
   B. Bald eagle
   C. Bluebird
   D. Blue Eagle

5. What country did Christopher Columbus think he was in when he discovered America?

   A. India
   B. Europe
   C. Amerigo
   D. Britain

6. What is "the Boston Tea Party?"
   A. A big tea party celebrated by the Indians
   B. A party celebrating the USA's Independence Day
   C. Important event when the colonists got together and dumped tea in the harbor
   D. A celebration for Christopher Columbus

7. When was the US Declaration of Independence from Britain signed?
   A. July 4, 1776
   B. July 14, 1776
   C. When the Boston Tea Party was ended
   D. July 4, 1556

8. If someone in the US gives you a buck, what do you have?
   A. A 10-cent coin
   B. A dollar
   C. A gift
   D. A greeting

9. Name one kind of music that started in America?
   A. Jazz
   B. Soul
   C. Country music
   D. All of the above

10. What is the name of the gold statuette Hollywood gives those who win awards for film?

    A. Emmy award
    B. MTV award
    C. Oscar
    D. Oliaster

11. What is American football's championship game called?

    A. The Soup Bowl
    B. The Big Series
    C. The Super Game
    D. The Super Bowl

ANSWERS

1-C, 2-A, 3-B, 4-B, 5-A, 6-C, 7-A, 8-B, 9-D, 10-C, 11-D

And to sum it all up...

SUMMARY OF THE TRIP

We had great fun, what a pity it is over ...

What were the most beautiful places and the best experiences of your journey?

> **First place –**

> **Second place –**

> **Third place –**

And now,

a difficult tasks—talk with your family and decide:

What did everyone enjoy most on the trip?

> **Grand Prize –**

Acknowledgment: All images are Shutterstock or public domain, except those mentioned below:
Attributions: 29ml-By Casta03 (Own work) [CC BY-SA 4.0 (http://creativecommons.org/licenses/by-sa/4.0)], via Wikimedia Commons; 29mcl-By David Shankbone (David Shankbone) [GFDL (http://www.gnu.org/copyleft/fdl.html) or CC-BY-SA-3.0 (http://creativecommons.org/licenses/by-sa/3.0/)], via Wikimedia Commons; 29mcr-By Glenn Francis uploaded by MyCanon (Britney Spears) [GFDL (http://www.gnu.org/copyleft/fdl.html) or CC BY-SA 4.0-3.0-2.5-2.0-1.0 (http://creativecommons.org/licenses/by-sa/4.0-3.0-2.5-2.0-1.0)], via Wikimedia Commons; 30ml-By Dave Gomez [CC BY-SA 4.0 (http://creativecommons.org/licenses/by-sa/4.0)], via Wikimedia Commons

Key: t=top;
b=bottom;
l=left;
r=right;
c=center;
m=main image;
bg=background